The Unofficial Harry Potter JOKE BOOK

The Unofficial Harry Potter Joke Book

Jokes, riddles, rhymes, trivia and tongue twisters for Muggles, wizards and witches alike.

ISBN 978-1-912511-82-2

Disclaimer

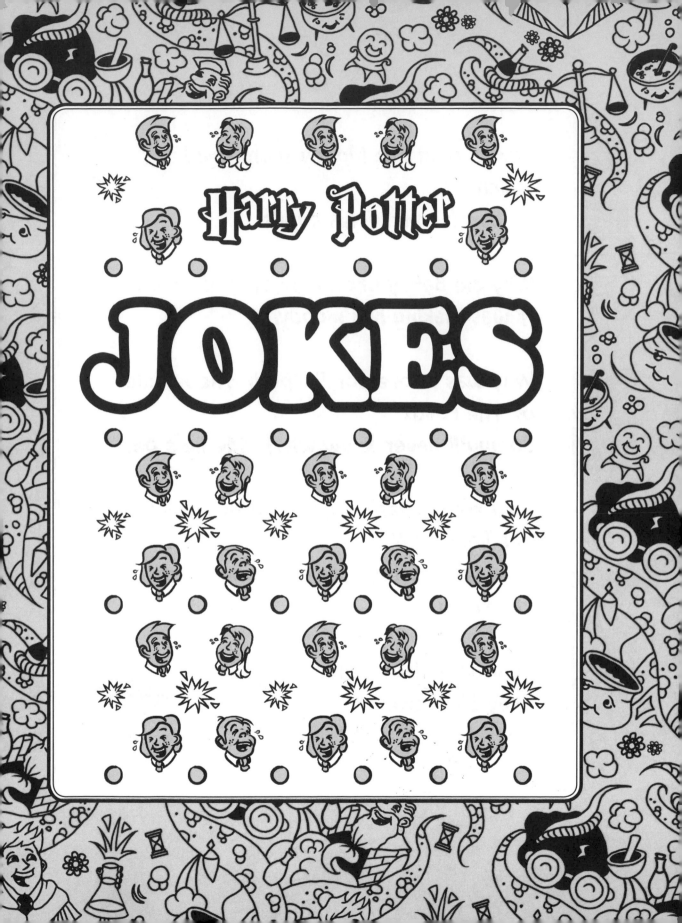

Harry Potter

JOKES

Why is Mad Eye Moody such a bad teacher?
He can't control his pupils.

Why did Barty Crouch Jr. stop drinking?
It was making him moody.

Why was Professor Snape in the middle of the road?
So you'll never know what side he's on.

How many wizards does it take to screw in a lightbulb?
Two. One to hold the bulb, one to rotate the room.

How do Malfoys enter a building?
They Slytherin.

Why couldn't Ron move his car?
It got stuck in a qui-ditch.

Why doesn't Voldemort wear glasses?
Nobody nose.

How do wizards get rid of rashes?
With quit-itch.

What happened to the Wizard with an upside-down nose?
Every time he sneezed his hat blew off.

Why did Neville Longbottom throw up in mid-air?
He gets broom-sick.

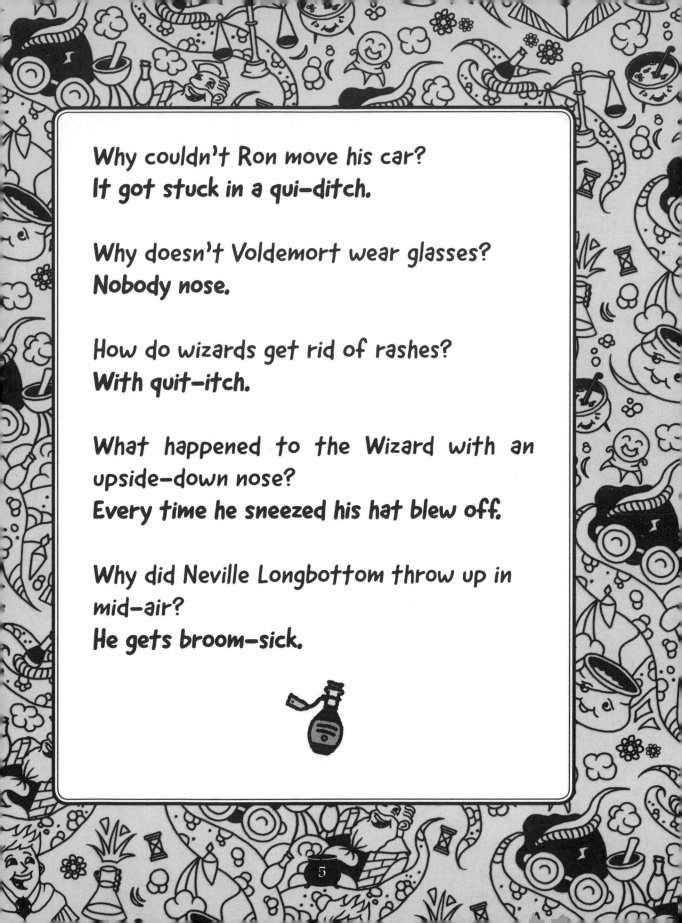

Knock knock!
Who's there?
Gryffin.
Gryffin who?
Gryffindor's locked, let me in!

What's a witches favorite coffee?
Espresso Patronum.

What did Harry Potter use to hide his
baldness?
A Hedwig.

Harry can't tell the difference between
his potion pot and his best friend.
They're both called Ron.

Why was Ron sent to the headmasters office?
He was cursing in class.

If your boyfriend looks like Oliver Wood he's probably a keeper.

What is the official wizarding language of postmen?
Parcel tongue.

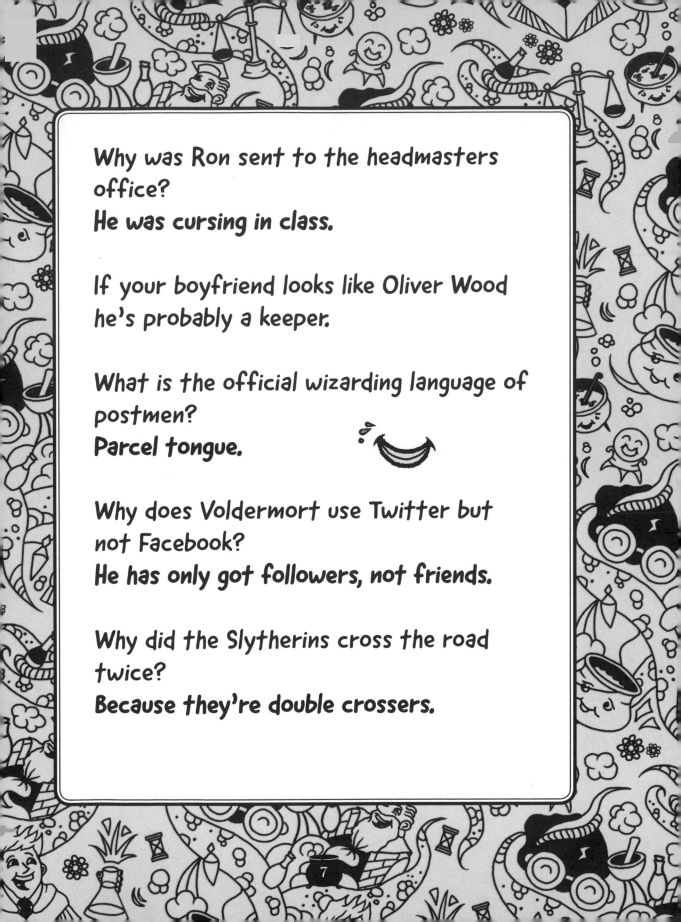

Why does Voldermort use Twitter but not Facebook?
He has only got followers, not friends.

Why did the Slytherins cross the road twice?
Because they're double crossers.

What medicine does a wizard take when they have a cold?
Floo powder.

Why does Neville have to use two toilets?
Because he has a Longbottom.

What do Death Eaters eat for breakfast?
Cruci-Os.

What do you call a young wizard who is planning to overthrow the ministry?
Harry Plotter.

What do you call a wizard headmaster who doesn't speak clearly?
Mumbledore.

If Ron and Harry abandoned Hermione
what would she be called?
The Lone Granger.

Why didn't Voldemort go to the Yule ball?
He had no-body to go with.

Where do you find Dumbledore's Army?
Up his sleevy.

What did Harry's godfather say when
Harry wouldn't stop pinching him?
"Stop that Harry, I'm Sirius."

What do you call a film about a boy
wizard and his disappointing photo's?
Harry Potter and the half-dark prints.

Which Minister for Magic has a car named after him?
Prius Thicknesse.

Knock knock!
Who's there?
Dumbledore.
Dumbledore who?
Dumb ol door isn't responding to my charms, open up!

Knock knock!
Who's there?
Harry.
Harry who?
Harry up and let me in! Your willow is whomping me!

Knock knock!
Who's there?
Hufflepuff.
Hufflepuff who?
I'll huff, I'll puff, I'll blow this door down.

What do wizards drink at a comedy show?
LOLyjuice potion.

How does the head of Gryffindor see
while she swims?
She uses McGonagoggles.

Why is it so hard to hear what's
happening inside the headmasters office?
Because it's got a mumble-dore.

How many Slytherins does it take to stir a cauldron?
Just one. He puts his wand in the cauldron and the world revolves around him.

A wizard walks into The Three Broomsticks and orders a forgetfulness potion. He turns to the witch next to him and asks, "So do I come here often?"

Who's Hermione's favourite singer?
Tina Time-Turner.

Harry got a great deal on a mortgage.
It was the sorcerer's loan.

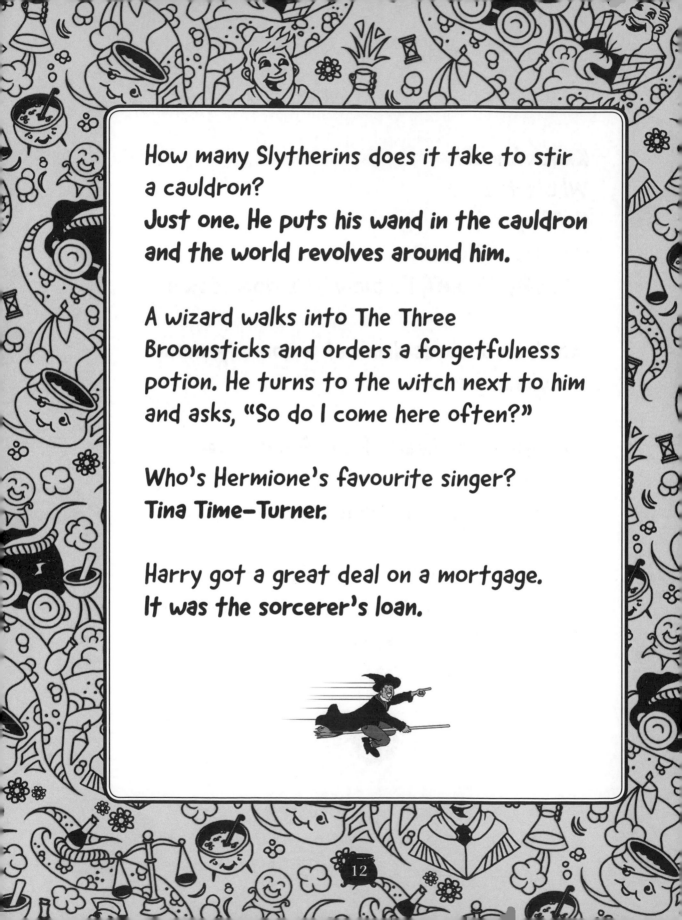

How do you get into Harry Potter's house?
Through the Gryffin-door of course!

Why'd Ron Weasley cross the road?
Somebody tossed a knut.

How did Harry feel during his time with the Dursleys?
He was in his own Privet hell!

What do you call a Hufflepuff with one brain cell?
Gifted.

What do you get when you cross a Ravenclaw with the infirmary?
Ill-literacy.

How many Slytherins does it take to screw a light bulb?

Five. One of them will screw the light bulb in, while the other four brag about their fathers' connections at the ministry and their Gringots vaults.

Knock, knock!

Who's there?

Oliver Wood.

Oliver Wood who?

Oliver Wood like to come in so can you open the door, please?

What does Professor McGonagall do every afternoon?

She has a little cat nap.

Why did Firenze miss a week of Divinations classes?
He was feeling rather horse.

What do you call a Headmaster of Hogwarts who keeps tripping on his cloak?
Stumbledore.

What do you call a Headmaster of Hogwarts who keeps the whole school up at night?
Dumblesnore.

How do they serve their salad in the Lupin household?
Using salad Tonks.

Who won the spell-ing bee?
Bumbledore.

What do Hogwarts professors get when they leave their jobs?
A severus package, of course!

Which Hogwarts master gets the blame for everything that goes wrong?
Professor Snape-goat!

What comes after Aberforth Dumbledore?
Aber-fifth Dumbledore.

What's Ollivander's favourite weekend activity?
Having a nice wand-er around, of course!

Why does Neville get his trousers made 'specially at Madam Malkin's?
His Longbottom!

Knock knock!
Who's there?
You know!
You know who?
Yeah, exactly.

How does Snape make his spaghetti bolognese?
With half-blood mince.

What advice would Pinocchio give to Lord Voldemort?
Voldy, you just have to lie to get a nose.

Why did Death Eaters cross the road?
The Dark Lord ordered it, of course.

What did Voldemort say when Wormtail asked if the Dark Lord would really rise again?
"Yes, but you may have to give me a hand."

What do you call a Dark Lord who has taken a job as an electrician?
Lord Volt-demort.

Why did Crabbe and Goyle cross the road?
They were following Draco, as always!

What does Harry Potter have that Voldemort doesn't?
A nose!

Why did Nearly Headless Nick and the Bloody Baron feel so terrible on Sunday morning?
They'd been to a party where there was nothing but spirits.

Knock Knock !
Who's There?
Oliver Wood.
Oliver Wood who?
Oliver Wood you just open the door!

Why do quidditch players travel on brooms?
It's hard to balance on a vacuum cleaner.

What was the name of Harry Potter's unsuccessful first rap single?
I got ninety-nine problems, but the snitch ain't one.

How did the Chudley Cannons' annual roast go?
Everyone was in snitches!

Which Hogwarts student do you think would help you practice Quidditch?
I think Oliver Wood.

How many wizards does it take to change a lightbulb?
Don't be silly, they'd never change a lightbulb, wizards don't use electricity!

What do you call a young wizard on a horse?
Harry Trotter.

Hey, did you hear about the witch who won the lottery?
Yeah! I heard she went totally knuts!

How many Seekers does it take to change a lightbulb?
Just one, and he gets a hundred and fifty points for it!

What do you call a wizard with a beard?
Hairy Potter.

What do you call a wizard with a cold?
Harry Snotter.

What do you get when you cross the Dark Lord with Harry Potter?
Dead.

How do Hawaiian wizards say 'hello'?
'Aloha-mora!'

What did the comedian say to the wizard?
Why so Sirius?

What's a potions teacher's favourite social media site?
Snape Chat!

How do you know if someone's a Pureblood?
Don't worry, they'll let you know.

So, Harry Potter and the Order of the Phoenix.
I guess that's when the books started getting... Dead Sirius.

What do aurorer's say when they eat tasty food?
It's Dawlish!

Which member of the Order of the Phoenix is always grouchy?
Alastor (Mad-Eye) Moody.

How do Deatheaters freshen their breath?
With De-mentos.

How do you get a mythical creature into your house?
Through the Gryffindor.

How does Aragog speak to his friends?
On the world wide web.

What does a Phoenix use to eat dinner?
Knives and Fawkes.

Why does Dobby keep criticizing himself?
He has low elf esteem.

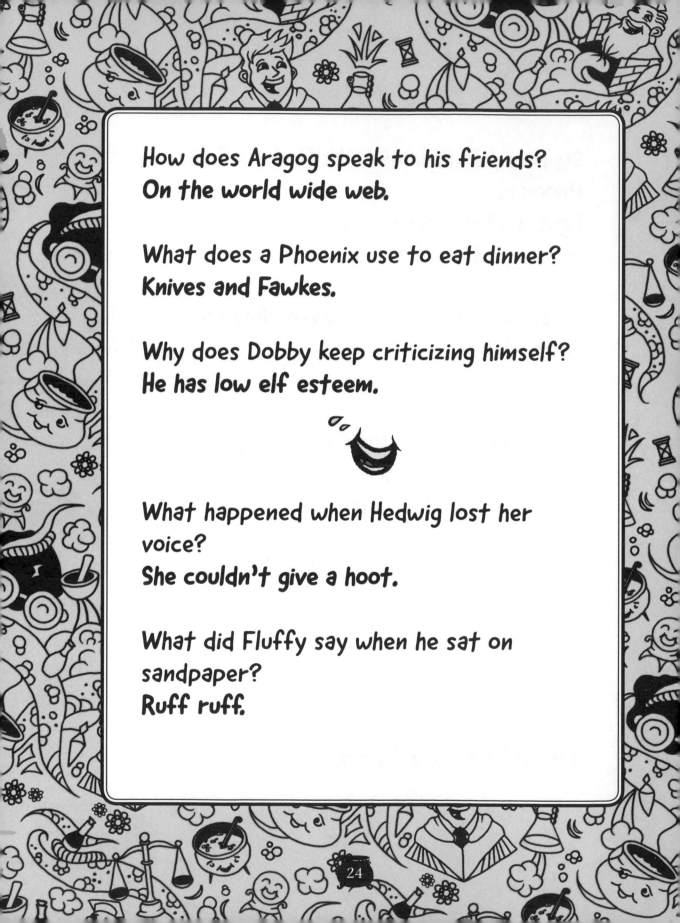

What happened when Hedwig lost her voice?
She couldn't give a hoot.

What did Fluffy say when he sat on sandpaper?
Ruff ruff.

What is Aragogs favourite day of the week?
Flyday.

Why isn't Fluffy a good dancer?
He has two left feet.

Why do you never see Dementors in Starbucks?
They won't drink Espresso Patronums.

What is Miss Grangers centaur name?
Hermio-neigh.

Why does Voldemort love Nagini?
She gives him hugs and hisses.

What's the difference between a comma and Crookshanks?

A comma is a pause at the end of a clause, and Crookshanks has claws at the end of his paws.

A muggle walks into the Hog's Head Inn with a frog on his shoulder.

The bartender says, "That's pretty cool, where'd you find it?"

"London," the frog croaks, "They've got thousands of them!"

How do goblins do gymnastics?

With a Gringots vault!

What does a turkey have in common with a Gringots bankteller?

They're both gobblin'!

Why did Firenze go all the way to Gambol and Japes?
They were having the sale of the Centaur-y!

What's a Dementor's favourite take-away?
An Azkebab.

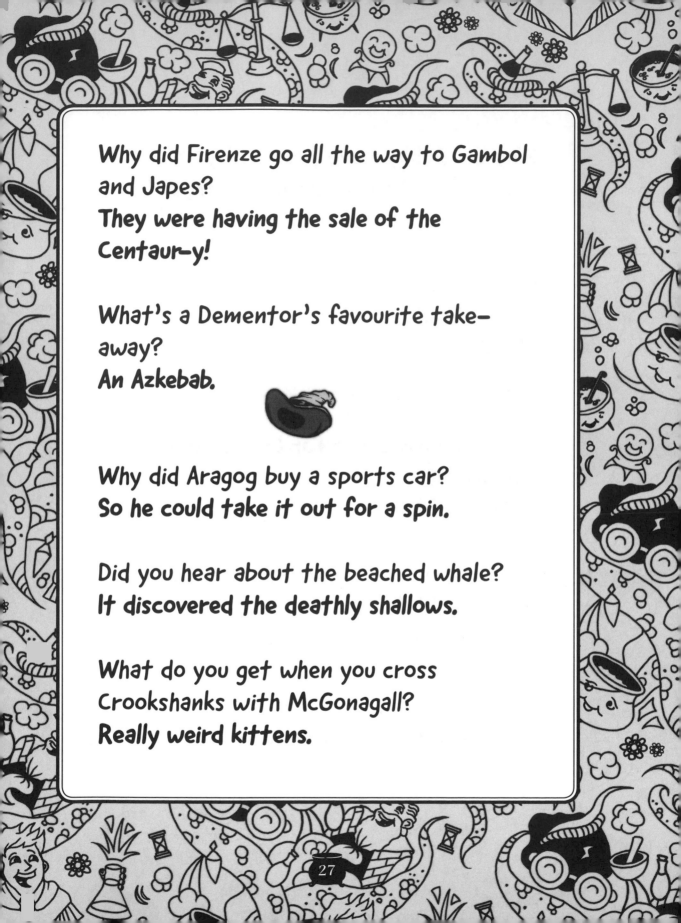

Why did Aragog buy a sports car?
So he could take it out for a spin.

Did you hear about the beached whale?
It discovered the deathly shallows.

What do you get when you cross Crookshanks with McGonagall?
Really weird kittens.

Why did Dobby leave the Malfoys'?
They valued their amazing wealth, but not their amazing elf!

On a scale of 1 to 10, how much of a Potterhead are you?
About 9¾.

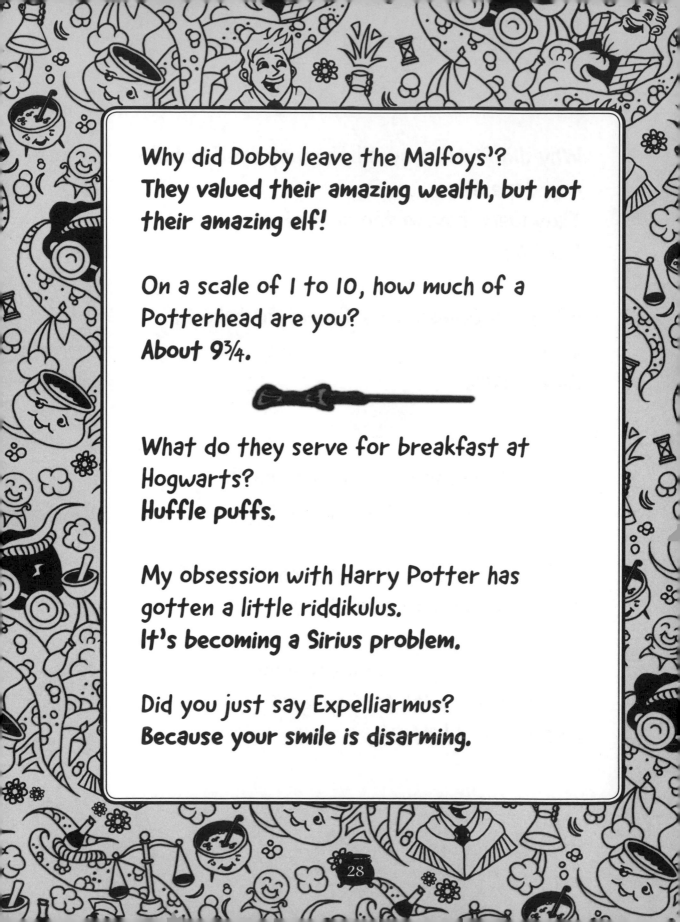

What do they serve for breakfast at Hogwarts?
Huffle puffs.

My obsession with Harry Potter has gotten a little riddikulus.
It's becoming a Sirius problem.

Did you just say Expelliarmus?
Because your smile is disarming.

Oh, so you don't get my Harry Potter jokes?
There must be some thing Ron with you.

You're so Muggle...
You thought Hogwarts was an illness only found in pigs.

What was everyone's favourite dance move at the Yule Ball?
The Shufflepuff.

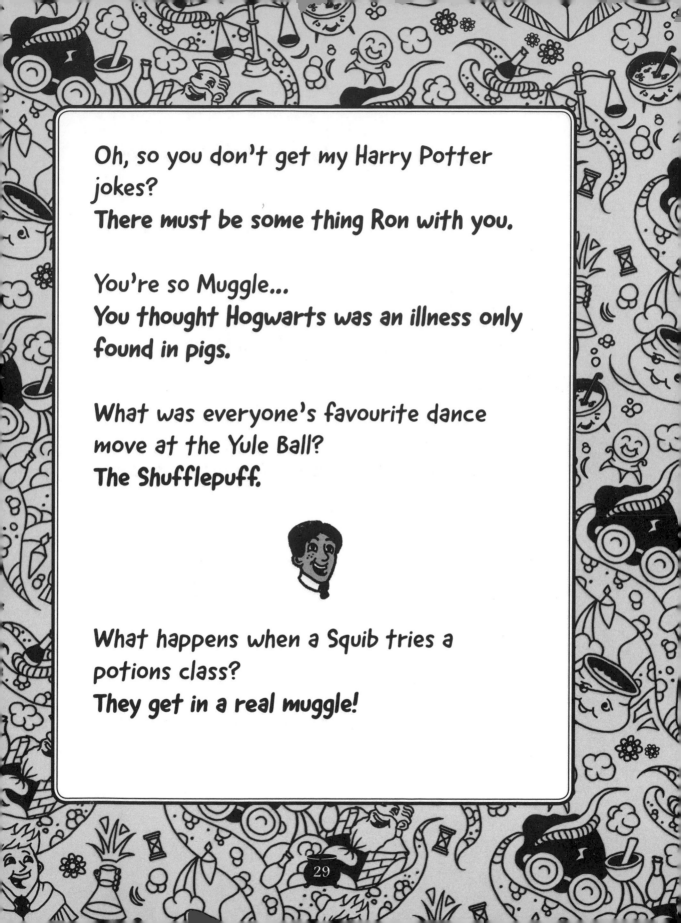

What happens when a Squib tries a potions class?
They get in a real muggle!

How many muggles does it take to screw in a lightbulb?
Just one. It's the only thing they're good for.

You're So Muggle...
You thought the floo network was on channel 54.

You're so Muggle...
You thought polyjuice potion was a sports drink.

What do you call a postman who can speak to packages?
A parcel-tongue.

You're so Muggle...
You thought the Swedish Shortsnout was in Abba.

You're so Muggle...
You thought the Chinese Fireball was a cocktail.

How do wizards feel in the Muggle world?
Like fish out of gillywater!

You're so Muggle...
You thought Diagon-alley was a direction.

Why do mafia bosses love Harry Potter?
Because he's the best at catching snitches!

Knock knock!
Who's there?
Wingardium Levio.
Wingardium Levio who?
It's Wingardivam Levi-O-SAAAA.

Why do wizards who drink polyjuice
potion deserve respect?
They're people two!

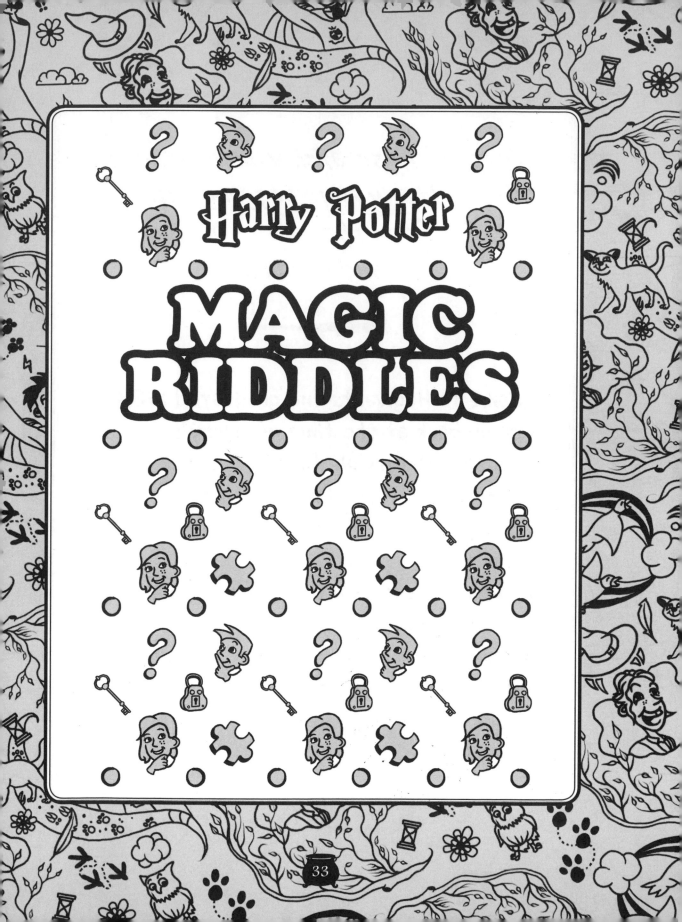

Harry Potter
MAGIC RIDDLES

Prepare to scratch your head with these utterly mind boggling, fiendish riddles from the halls of Hogwarts and beyond.

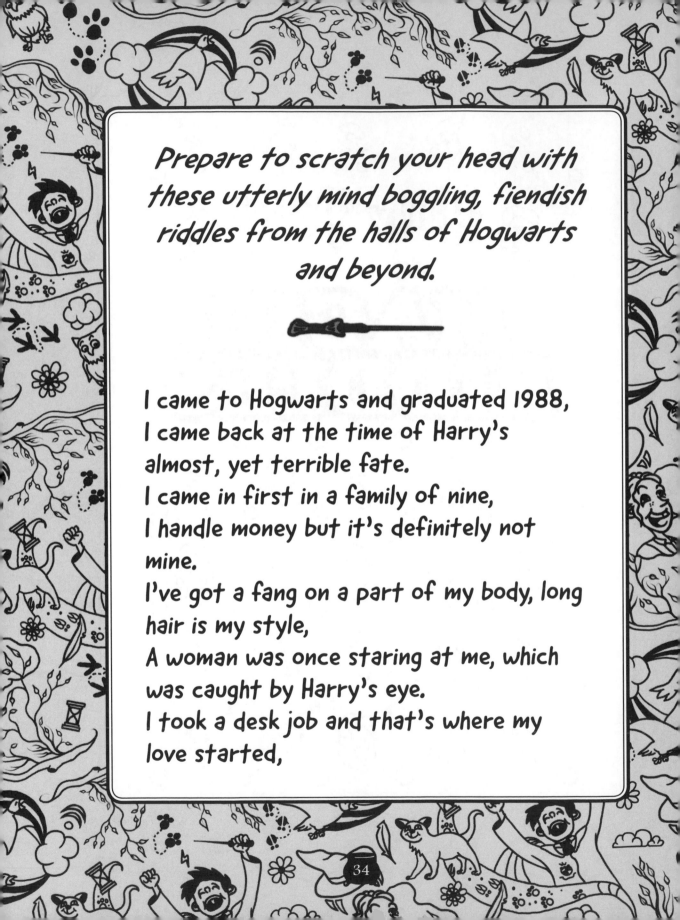

I came to Hogwarts and graduated 1988,
I came back at the time of Harry's almost, yet terrible fate.
I came in first in a family of nine,
I handle money but it's definitely not mine.
I've got a fang on a part of my body, long hair is my style,
A woman was once staring at me, which was caught by Harry's eye.
I took a desk job and that's where my love started,

I joined the Order of which cannot be parted.

I wear dragonhide on my feet, muggle clothes is what I've got,

My charm would outwit anyone, do you think they have not?

I respect my family with pride, unlike a dear brother that is so uncool,

One quality we share is that we were both Prefects at our dear old school.

Who am I?

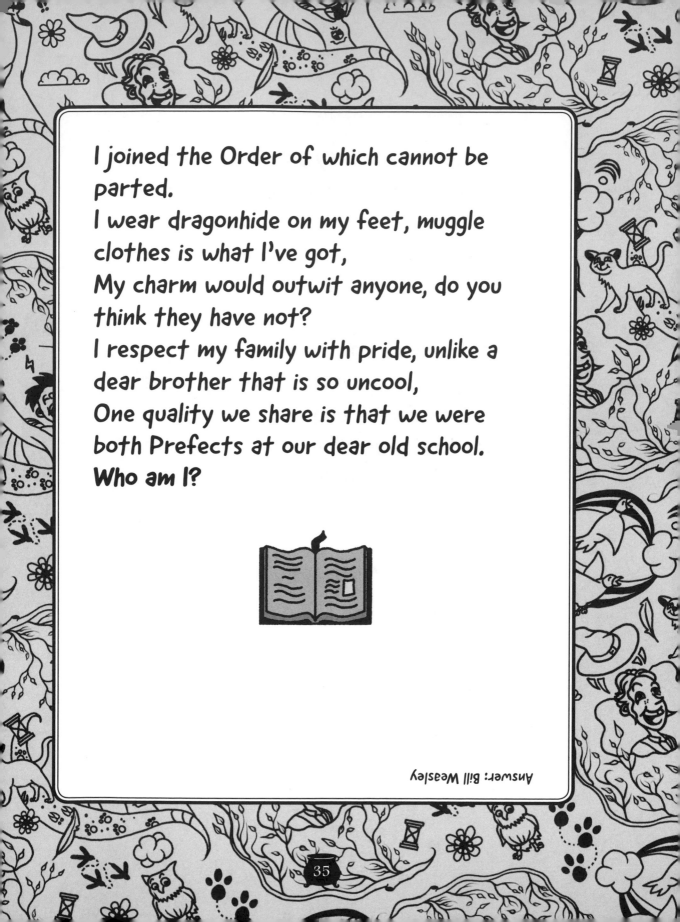

I'm someone you may possibly meet,
on an average day, in an average street.
He saw me before he knew what he was
and twice I helped people pass through
Voldy's claws. **Who am I?**

The Marauders consider me weak.
Am I a man or a mouse? Squeak, squeak!
Ratted on James and Lily,
I guess that was silly.
And now I'm a one-handed freak.
Who am I?

On film I'm a strapping young buck.
In the books I walk like a duck.
I'm the world's best seeker,
But not a great speaker
And Hermy-own-ninny I'd like to date.
Who am I?

The Prophet prints nothing but ill.
Of the people I quote with my quill.
A bug getting news,
Granger outed my ruse
Blackmailed me and told me to chill.
Who am I?

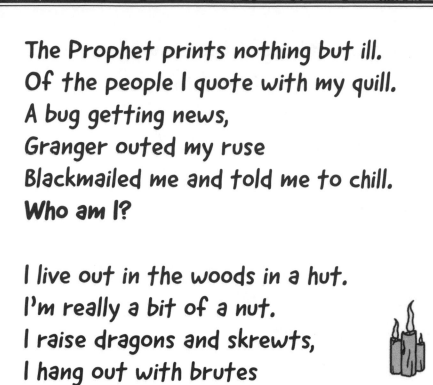

I live out in the woods in a hut.
I'm really a bit of a nut.
I raise dragons and skrewts,
I hang out with brutes
And my mother's a giant, so what?
Who am I?

Look, am I really that bad?
I'm less of a jerk than my dad.
I played Harry's foil,
Just like Crabbe and Goyle.
I'm the number one Slytherin cad.
Who am I?

I thought J.K. thought I was swell.
She was just biding time ' til I fell.
She ended my life,
With Lestrange's thrown knife.
I guess I'll see Rowling in hell!
Who am I?

My spell casting skills are quite keen.
My library visits routine.
I've got bushy hair,
I'm totally square.
I'm the brightest witch you've ever see.
Who am I?

If you're looking for evil I'm it.
But I really screwed up, to wit.
I tried to kill Harry,
He used love to parry.
I instead killed myself like a twit.
Who am I?

Answers: Dobby | Hermione | Voldemort

38

I have a strong urge to expound.
On the way I was easily downed.
In dueling I failed,
And I sailed through the Veil.
I should have just stayed as a hound.
Who am I?

I was the pride of those who owned me
and a murder sealed my fate.
For years my true identity went unknown
and my end was brought by the one
who stopped me from finishing off my
foe.
Who am I?

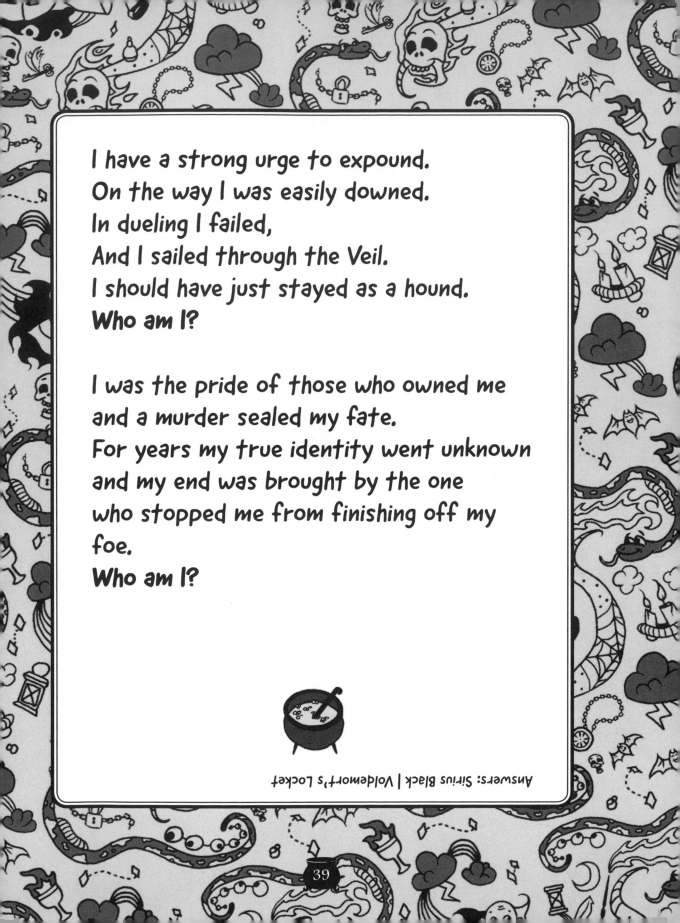

I have no wings, but I like to fly.
I can go fast, but no brain have I.
I come in a wide range, and play in some sports.
I break quite easily, if I smash into walls.
Who am I?

Answer: A broomstick

Harry Potter RHYMES

Cunning and clever withcraft & wizardry have been used to compile these crafty rhymes.

An orphaned wizard boy named Harry,
With a wave of his wand could parry,
The schemes of his foes,
Which lessened his woes.
But still... his adventure was scary!

Their once was a Weasley named Ron,
Who had trouble with robes he would don.
His heart was pure,
But he acted demure,
When his girlfriend called him Won-Won.

Herminone's at the top of her class,
But don't you dare give her no sass.
Or her wand she'll flick,
To show you a trick,
And you may find yourself in a cast.

To Harry, Dumbledore was a mentor,
With a presence that's hard to ignore.
He may seem docile,
But he's no fossil,
For he can easily stop a Dementor!

Hagrid may appear most compliant,
For to his friends, he is very reliant.
Due to his size,
You'll come to realize,
That he's huge, for he's actually half
giant!

Voldemort's motives can never be tamed.
To his enemies he always brings shame.
For his power is strong,
And his reach quite long,
Hence he's called, "He-who-must-not-
be-named."

Harry's love turned out to be Ginny,
Who certainly wasn't a ninny.
She stood by his side,
To live or to die,
Harry's one lucky wizard, isn't he?

Young Neville, though timid of heart,
When it comes to plants, he is smart.
His toad is Trevor,
And with loyalty ever,
From his friends, he never will part.

Draco Malfoy had very little merit,
When his father, he started to parrot.
His big disgrace,
Is once he lost face,
When Mad-Eye turned him into a ferret!

Oh the tragic, sad tale of poor Snape,
Who hides feelings behind his black cape.
His heart set on Lily,
Was not willy-nilly;
From such love, he could not escape.

Fred and George have mirth with no bounds.
Their pranks are the stuff of renown.
Their Marauder's Map,
Takes only a tap,
To display all who walk on the grounds.

There's no item like the Sorting Hat,
Who'll sit on your head and then chat.
Your house he'll pick,
It's really quite slick,
Then off you go to your new habitat.

Ollivander's wands are a wonder.
He assigns them all without blunder.
But the spells you cast
—Don't say them too fast—
Or you may rend yourself all asunder!

Gryffindor is a house for the brave,
And for chivalry; not known for knaves.
Scarlet and gold,
With lion bold,
Though its members may not always
behave.

Hufflepuff, of the yellow and black,
For true loyalty, it has a knack.
With no swagger,
And an animal badger,
From other houses, it'll never take flack.

Ravenclaw, know for wisdom and smarts,
Unto others, much knowledge imparts.
Bronze and blue,
With eagle true,
From their books, they never wish to
depart.

Slytherin, of the silver and green,
Have minds that are ever quite keen.
So watch your back,
Or you they'll attack,
For their morals are truly obscene.

Harry's godfather was Sirius Black.
He was framed for a most heinous act.
To jail he went,
Where years he spent,
For a crime against those he didn't attack.

Over Azkaban, Dementors do watch.
Their vigilance is truly top notch.
Don't draw their gaze,
Or you'll start to phase,
And they'll drain your soul with a touch.

Poor Nearly Headless Nick is a ghost,
With the kindness of a genuine host,
Yet deep down inside,
A part of him cries,
For the Headless Hunt he wants to join most.

Padfoot, Wormtail, Moony, and Prongs,
Had a friendship to which they belonged.
Yet one strayed;
The others betrayed,
After which, everything else all went wrong.

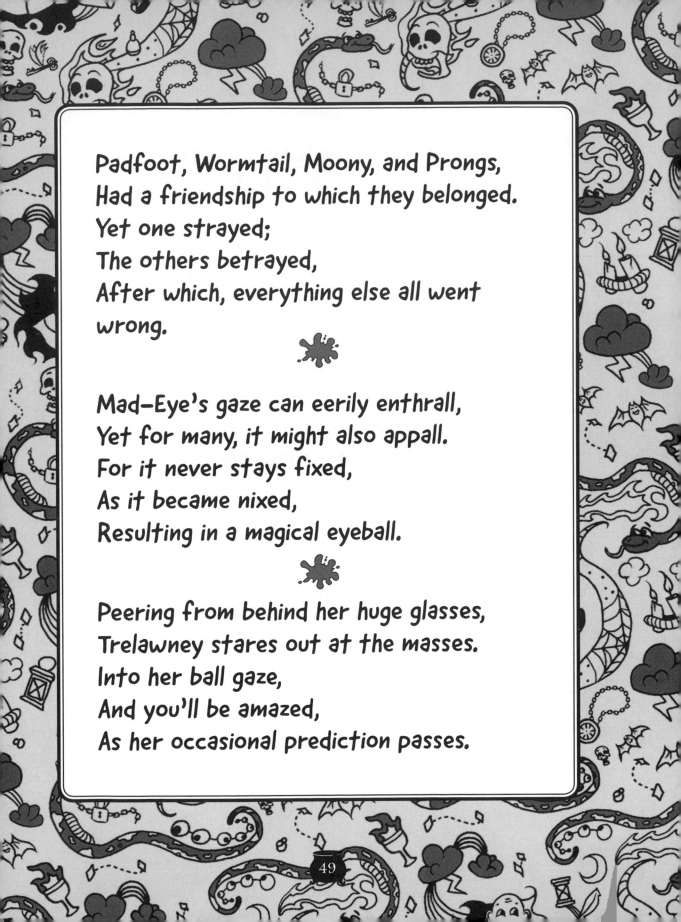

Mad–Eye's gaze can eerily enthrall,
Yet for many, it might also appall.
For it never stays fixed,
As it became nixed,
Resulting in a magical eyeball.

Peering from behind her huge glasses,
Trelawney stares out at the masses.
Into her ball gaze,
And you'll be amazed,
As her occasional prediction passes.

Basilisks are vile creatures of dark;
Never confront one on a lark.
From them, do turn,
Or you will soon learn,
That their gaze makes your soul to embark.

Roses are red
Violets are blue
I thought Voldermort was ugly
But then I saw you!

Dumbledore's Phoenix named Fawkes,
Often causes others to gawk.
With tears to heal,
Wounds congeal,
But take care of its cry when it squawks!

Nagini is Voldemort's snake,
Whose gaze from yours never will break.
She'll deftly slide,
Up to your side,
For her appetite can never be slaked.

Peter Pettigrew turned into a rat,
Scurrying this way and that.
When he was attacked,
A finger he lacked,
So he now has to avoid every cat!

Harry's love turned out to be Ginny,
Who certainly wasn't a ninny.
She stood by his side,
To live or to die,
Harry's one lucky wizard, isn't he?

Luna lives in her own unique space,
With clothes of a distinctive taste,
With her heart true,
She will subdue,
Those who stand up for evil with haste.

If you ever send mail, use an owl.
For they are a magnificent fowl.
But you'd better,
Avoid a letter,
That's red, for it'll soon start to howl!

Thestrals, to the most watchful eye,
Cannot be seen from low or on high.
Still, you just might,
See one in flight,
If you witness a person's demise.

Felix Felicis, or "Liquid Luck,"
Makes you a hero; never a schmuck.
One tiny bit,
Will make you fit,
For a day that will leave you awestruck.

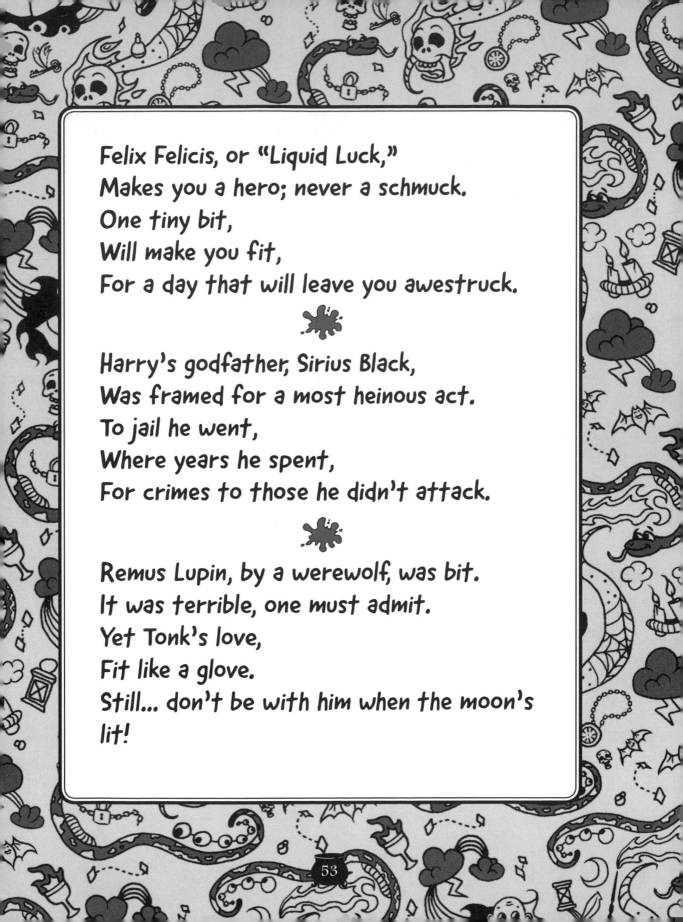

Harry's godfather, Sirius Black,
Was framed for a most heinous act.
To jail he went,
Where years he spent,
For crimes to those he didn't attack.

Remus Lupin, by a werewolf, was bit.
It was terrible, one must admit.
Yet Tonk's love,
Fit like a glove.
Still... don't be with him when the moon's
lit!

Xenophilius is one who insists,
(Even if you find him amiss)
That Nargles hide there,
Or indeed, anywhere,
Because he swears they truly exist!

James Potter proved to be quite a
scamp,
Around his friends, he did like to prank.
His boyish charm,
Left Lily unarmed,
And he grew up to become a true champ.

Sweet Lily Potter had only one son,
And too soon, her life was undone.
Yet her love stood,
For all that was good;
By her sacrifice, love finally won.

McGonagall is known to be strict.
In her class, do not attempt tricks.
Or egos she'll bruise,
And you'll quickly lose,
Several house points, as they will get
nicked!

Dolores Umbridge makes your skin crawl,
As she giggles with unabashed gall.
Give her attention,
Or risk detention,
And upon your own hand you will scrawl.

If your senses begin to take leave,
While your anger does equally seethe,
Then he will be happy,
At making you crabby,
As all you can do is yell, "Peeves!"

A sport for both wizard and witch,
Is the popular game of Quidditch.
Do try to score,
But teams get more,
When a flash of gold reveals the Snitch!

Harry proved to those who act snobby,
That house-elves (with legs rather wobbly),
Can be a true friend,
Who'll last to the end...
Such is the sad story of Dobby.

The Grey Lady is a ghost who saw,
Her mom's diadem, and craved it all.
It led to her death,
And her last breath,
For she is Helena Ravenclaw.

Beware the beans of Bertie Bott.
Some eat a few, some eat a lot.
So try a taste,
But not with haste,
For a nasty flavor may be snot!

A dark magic item, the Horcrux,
Will leave your poor soul in a flux.
Avoid casting one,
For if it's undone,
Your essence will then become stuck.

Flitwick, a true master of charms,
Has short little legs and stout arms.
When evil attacked,
He had a knack,
For setting up Hogwarts' alarms.

Kreacher, a dubious house-elf,
Kept the dark locket up on a shelf.
It wouldn't break,
Making him ache,
And incredibly mad at himself.

Filch and Mrs. Norris are a pair.
At every poor student they stare.
If you've done wrong,
To you they'll throng,
Chasing you up and down every stair.

To copy someone, have the notion,
Of making some Polyjuice Potion.
Avoid hair of cat,
Or you'll become that,
As Hermione, and cause a commotion!

Wizarding families are not glib,
With a child who's born as a squib.
They can't do magic,
Which they find tragic,
So others may taunt them and rib.

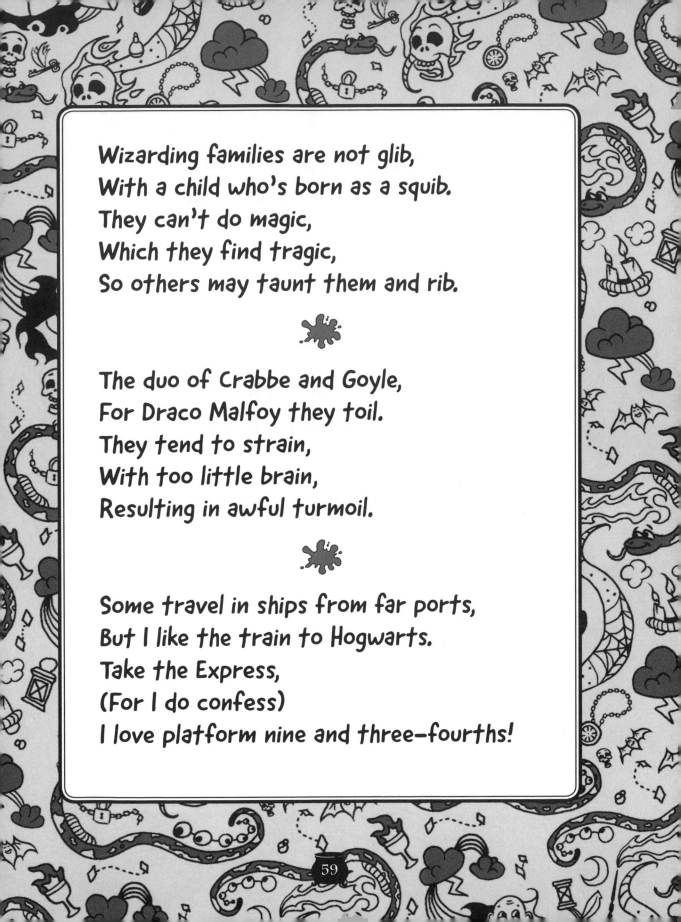

The duo of Crabbe and Goyle,
For Draco Malfoy they toil.
They tend to strain,
With too little brain,
Resulting in awful turmoil.

Some travel in ships from far ports,
But I like the train to Hogwarts.
Take the Express,
(For I do confess)
I love platform nine and three-fourths!

Mighty centaurs lurk in the wood,
Haughty and proud, yet still good.
Gazing at stars,
All from afar,
Indeed, they are misunderstood.

To make your name most permanent,
Win the grand Triwizard's Tournament!
Complete each trial,
With deft and style,
And your school you'll then represent!

There's no safer place on the earth,
Than Gringotts to store all your worth.
The goblins there,
Will hide your wares,
And thieves will give it a wide berth.

Ron and Harry drove a flying car,
Which actually went very far.
It fell in a tree,
Then got hit madly,
Which probably gave them some scars!

Cedric Diggory ran for the prize,
However, he did not realize,
It was a Portkey,
Which made him flee,
And led to his untimely demise.

Aragog is one massive spider,
Who doesn't like any outsider.
He loves his kind.
His webs can bind.
If he nabs you, his grin will get wider!

A youth by the name of Tom Riddle,
Did not, his thumbs, merely twiddle.
With a will strong,
Gathered a throng;
He refused to live life in the middle.

A sad ghost known as Moaning Myrtle,
Had many obstacles to hurdle.
She wails in the bath,
But beware her wrath,
For her screams will make your blood curdle.

If you ever prepare for Yule Ball,
Be sure that you give it your all.
Do dress well,
Act real swell,
And don't be a flower on the wall!

To breathe well in water (if you need),
Get yourself some green Gillyweed.
Dive in the lake,
A gasp you'll take,
And then through the waters you'll proceed.

Buckbeak is a fine hippogriff,
Who flies high over any wide rift.
Yet be wary,
He is scary,
If you cross him and get in a tiff.

When a wizard tries to Apparate,
It causes him to dissipate.
But in a pinch,
You just might splinch,
Causing your body to separate!

Horace Slughorn, professor of old,
Was a timid man; not very bold.
Tom, he taught,
And later caught,
In a tale he'd have rather not told.

Because Hermione's a great learner,
To her was trusted a Time-Turner.
If used too much,
Becomes a crutch,
At which point, professors would spurn her.

Hagrid had a dragon named Norbert.
Though small, fiery breath he could spurt.
Watch his flame,
Or you're to blame,
For allowing yourself to get hurt.

Fang is Hagrid's wondrous boarhound,
Who's large, with a grand barking sound.
Mind his drool,
Don't be a fool,
As his jump can drop you to the ground.

Ye Olde Hog's Head is where to draw near.
Order what you'd like with a cheer.
Do not dismay,
Else you just may,
Request a tall mug of butterbeer!

A Patronus is a powerful spell,
With effects you can definitely tell.
For it will feature,
A distinct creature,
Especially when you cast it quite well.

The Mirror of Erised is unique,
Revealing some things most oblique.
What you long,
It will prolong,
But with an element of mystique.

Giants can be terrible foes,
Giving people plenty of woes.
At over a ton,
Young Grawp is one,
For both he and Hagrid are bros.

Unforgivable curses are forbidden.
Of them, many wizards have written.
Only the vile,
Would dare smile,
And with them be completely smitten.

The Ministry of Magic is where,
Many laws and trials are laid bare.
With secrets doors,
And shiny floors,
If trapped inside, it is a nightmare.

A reporter named Rita Skeeter;
Trust me—you'd rather not meet her.
With her quill,
And strong will,
Out of a story, you cannot cheat her!

Hedwig is an amazing bird;
An owl, who is never absurd.
Mail she'll carry,
To her friend Harry;
Her loyalty cannot be deterred.

Few are as vile as Bellatrix,
Upon you, her gaze will transfix.
An evil spell,
She knows quite well;
Avoid her or you'll be in a fix.

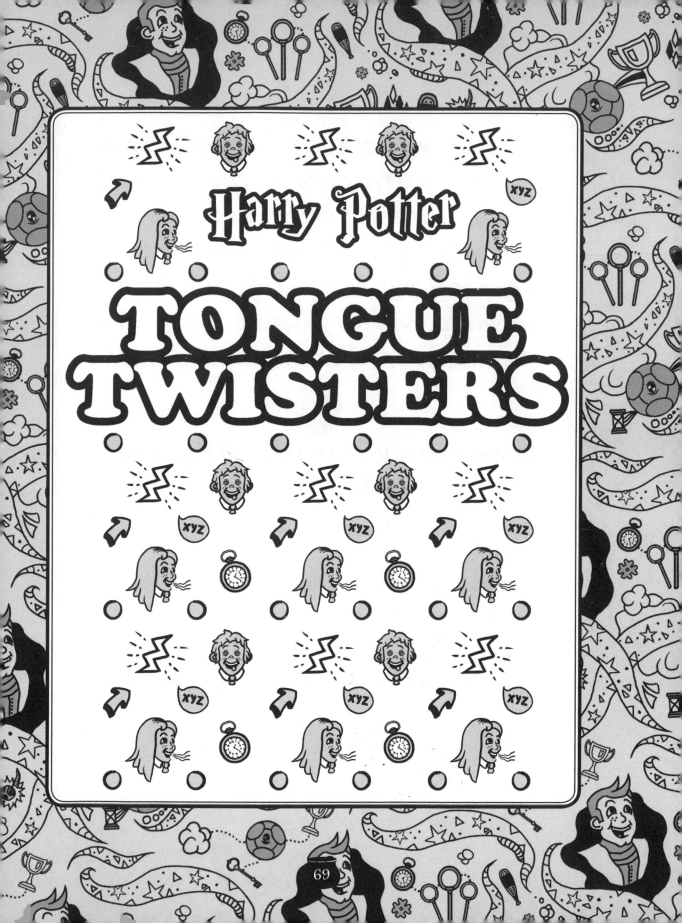

These words are not for wafflers as tongue twisters can be tricky. Try to say it twice or three times in a row ... remember it's not just how fast you say them, but how clearly too! For the ultimate test try saying them with ton-tongue toffee. Utterly impossible.

Moaning Myrtle must now mutter, much of matters marking monsters.

Hapless Hagrid has a hut.
Huddled in it hatched a hatchling.
Hoping Hagrid has a hint,
That hugging hatchlings hurts your hands!

Filch filches filthy filth.

Quirinus Quirrel quivered quite quickly.

Filius Flitwick fought off phantoms.

Dudley Dursley doesn't dare
Deride a Dementor, does he?

Slithering sly snake sapped stern Severus
Snape.

Fearsome Fluffy fears flighty flutes.

Padma Patil poured a pot of potent potions.
A pot of potent potions, Padma Patil poured.
If Padma Patil poured a pot of potent potions,
How many potent potions, did Padma Patil pour?

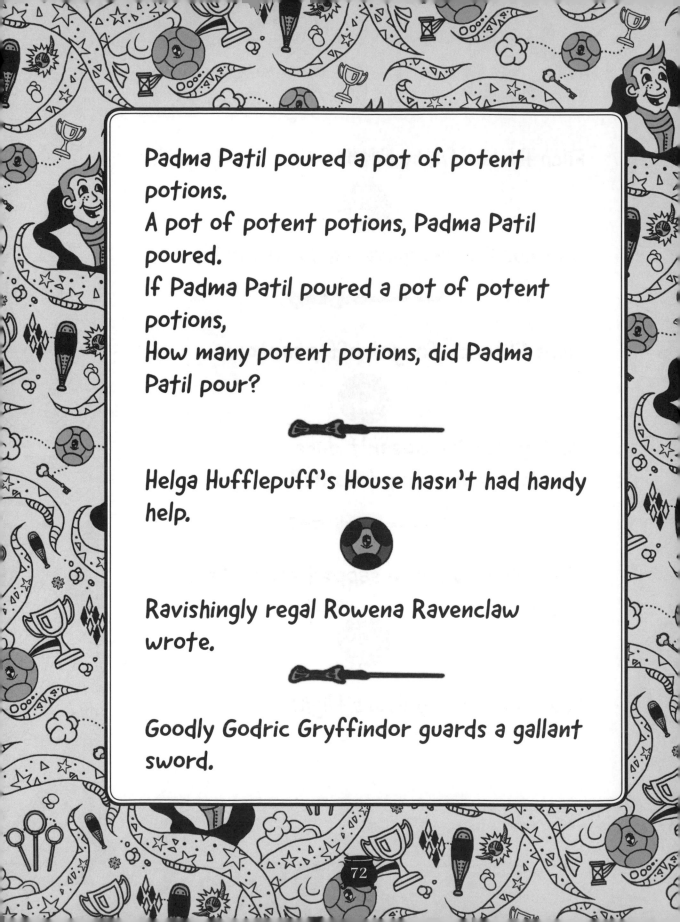

Helga Hufflepuff's House hasn't had handy help.

Ravishingly regal Rowena Ravenclaw wrote.

Goodly Godric Gryffindor guards a gallant sword.

Sly Salazar Slytherin shrewdly speaks to slithering snakes.

Minerva's magic mainly morphs mammals.

Durmstrang's Krum almost won.

Fumble Grumble Humble Lore,
Mumble Jumble Drumble Store,
Crumble Rumble Tumble More,
Stumble Bumble Dumbledore!

Mundungus hung fungus and sung a fun rumpus.

Muggles may not muster magic;
Making Monday mornings mundane.

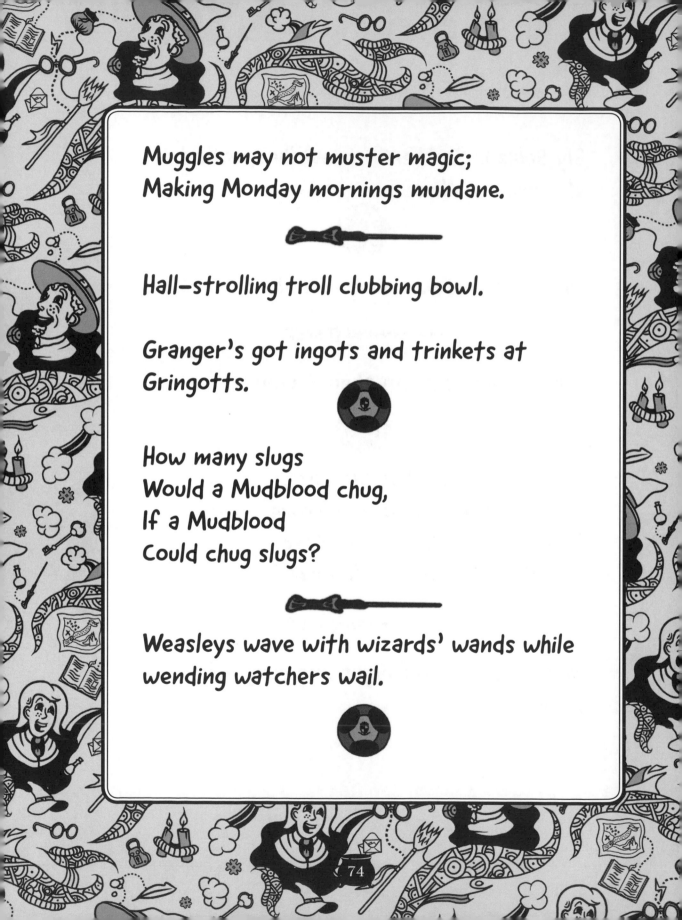

Hall—strolling troll clubbing bowl.

Granger's got ingots and trinkets at
Gringotts.

How many slugs
Would a Mudblood chug,
If a Mudblood
Could chug slugs?

Weasleys wave with wizards' wands while
wending watchers wail.

Harry Potter

TRIVIA

1. What is Mr Filch's first name?

2. Which members of order of the Phoenix are at The Burrow when it is burnt down by Death Eaters?

3. What is the name of the Ministry of Magic employee that Ron impersonates using Polyjuice Potion?

4. Who do Harry, as Albert Runcorn, and Hermione , as Mafalda Hopkirk, run into in an elevator at the Ministry of Magic?

5. What relation are Albus and Aberforth Dumbledore?

6. Who wears the symbol of the Deathly Hallows around their neck at the wedding of Bill and Fleur?

7. Which Weasley brother first owns Scabbers as a pet?

8. What position does Krum play on the Bulgarian Quidditch team?

9. Luna's father is the editor of which newspaper?

10. Which students does Harry save from the burning Room of Requirement after he has found the Horcrux diadem?

11. Viktor Krum is selected by the Goblet of Fire as the Triwizard champion for which school?

12. What department in the Ministry of Magic does Barty Crouch head up when the Triwizard Tournament occurs?

13. According to Griphook, who put the fake sword of Gryffindor inside Bellatrix Lestrange's vault?

14. Harry first apparates alongside whom?

15. What is Hermione's middle name?

16. Who saves Harry from drowning in the frozen lake in the Forest of Dean?

17. Who is the Half-Blood Prince?

18. Gwenog Jones is the captain of which Quidditch team?

19. What is the name of Harry's second son?

20. What is Gregorovitch's profession?

21. Who does Kingsley Shacklebolt act as a bodyguard for?

22. Why is Dobby able to apparate in and out of Malfoy Manor?

23. What form does Professor Snape's Patronus take?

24. What does Madame Maxime tell Hagrid that her horses drink?

25. What is the name of the creature that Luna describes as invisible and capable of floating into your ears and making your brain go fuzzy?

26. What two creatures does Voldemort use in the battle of Hogwarts aside from Dementors?

27. What comical touch does Ron give his Boggart spider?

28. Who is Hagrid buying when Professor Slughorn and Harry pay him a visit?

29. What is Harry's owl called?

30. What is Hagrid's half-brother's name?

31. What is the Black family's house elf called?

32. What creature does Mad-Eye moody use to demonstrate the Unforgiveable Curses on?

33. What animal tries to attack Harry, Ron and Hermione outside the Shrieking Shack?

34. What animals deliver post in the wizarding world?

35. What creature grabs Harry's hand when he tries to take water from the lake to give to Professor Dumbledore in the Horcrux cave?

36. Dolores Umbridge insults what magical creature in front of Harry and Hermione in the Forbidden Forest?

37. Aside from the Riddikulus charm, what else finishes a Boggart

38. A Hippogriff has the body, hind legs and tail of a horse, and the wings and head of a what?

39. Who dies whilst escaping from Malfoy Manor?

40. What Petrified animal do Harry, Ron and Hermione find hanging by her tail in a corridor?

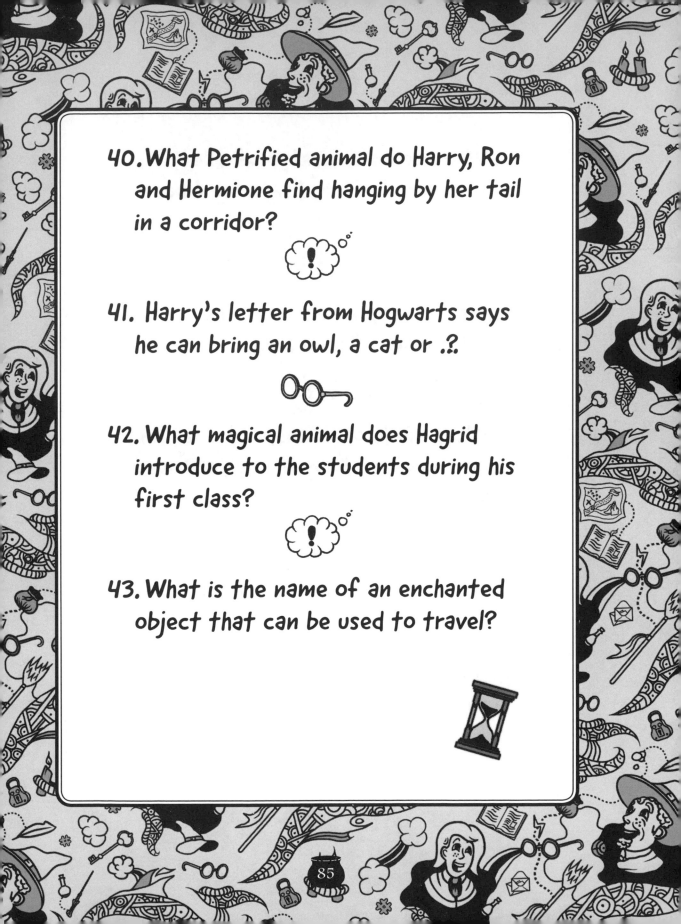

41. Harry's letter from Hogwarts says he can bring an owl, a cat or .?.

42. What magical animal does Hagrid introduce to the students during his first class?

43. What is the name of an enchanted object that can be used to travel?

44. Who becomes master of the Elder Wand after disarming Albus Dumledore?

45. What two powers does the Philosophers Stone hold?

46. What mode of transport does Hagrid use to deliver baby Harry to Privet Drive?

47. What sweets does Bertie Bott make?

48. What component is in both Harry and Voldemort's wands?

49. What is the name of the book that includes a story about the Deathly Hallows?

50. What is the core of Lucius Malfoy's wand?

51. What is a Pensieve used for?

52. What is the headline of the newspaper Harry reads on the Knight Bus?

53. The Minister of Magic personally delivers gifts bequeathed by Albus Dumbledore to which three characters?

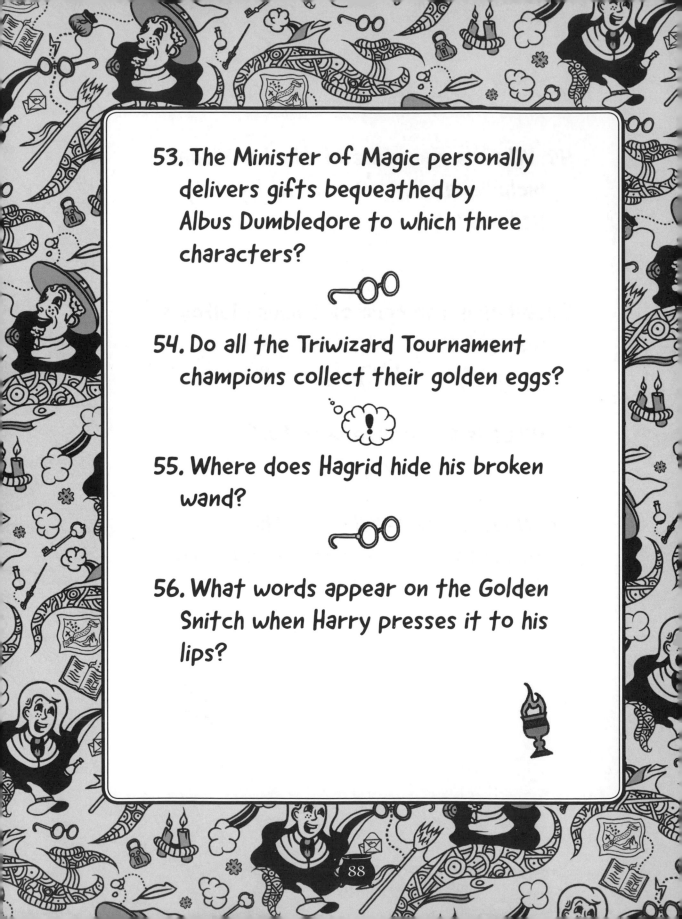

54. Do all the Triwizard Tournament champions collect their golden eggs?

55. Where does Hagrid hide his broken wand?

56. What words appear on the Golden Snitch when Harry presses it to his lips?

57. What initials appear on the fake Horcrux?

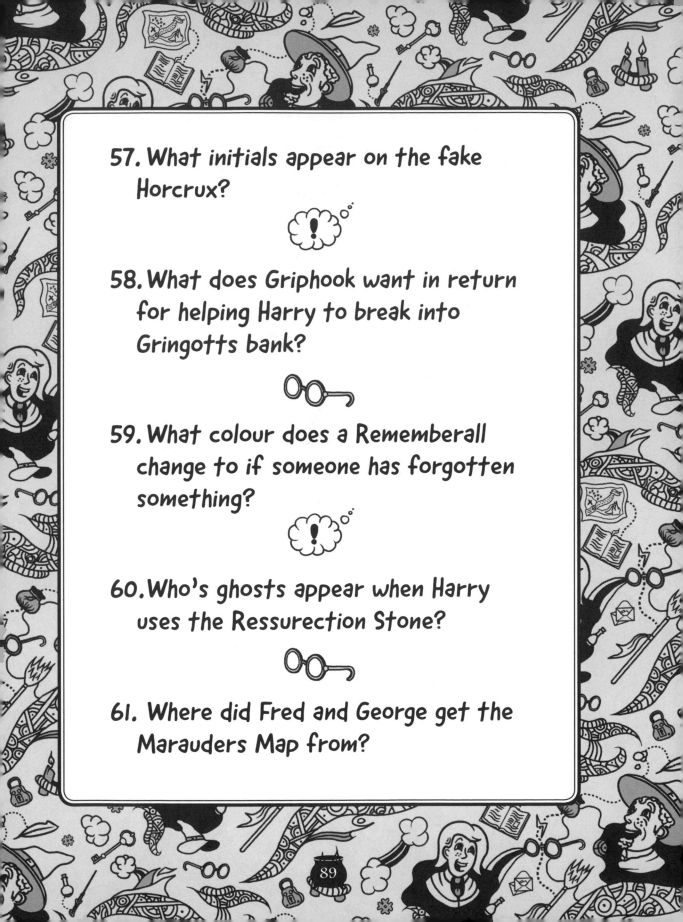

58. What does Griphook want in return for helping Harry to break into Gringotts bank?

59. What colour does a Rememberall change to if someone has forgotten something?

60. Who's ghosts appear when Harry uses the Ressurection Stone?

61. Where did Fred and George get the Marauders Map from?

62. What object is Horace Slughorn disguised as when Harry first meets him?

63. What household object shows the location and status of each Weasley family member?

64. What charm does Hermione use to open a locked door when running from Filch?

65. Who tries to enter their names into the Goblet of Fire after using an Ageing Potion?

66. What spell does Hermione cast on Harry when they are caught by Snatchers?

67. What professor calls Harry 'Prince of Potions'?

68. What ingredient does Hermione use in the Polyjuice potion that transforms her into Bellatrix Lestrange?

69. What is the incantation for the spell that smashes objects into tiny pieces?

70. What is the spell being taught in Professor Flitwicks Charms class when the students are learning how to levitate a feather?

71. What spell gets Harry into trouble with the Ministry of Magic?

72. What spell does Harry use to break the ice on the Frozen Lake whilst trying to retrieve the sword of Gryffindor?

73. What is the spell Legilimens used for?

74. What charm does Hermione use on the Death Eaters in a London café?

75. What colour streams from a wand performing the Killing Curse?

76. What is the Trace used for?

77. Who casts the Fiendfyre spell in the room of requirement?

78. What animal is Dolores Umbridge's Patronus?

79. What potion do the Order take and why when rescuing Harry from Privet Drive ?

80. What spell does Harry cast against Voldemort during their graveyard duel?

81. Who leaves chocolate laced with Love Potion intended for Harry, but it gets eaten by Ron?

82. What spell is used by Hermione to open Sirius Black's cell in the Dark Tower of Hogwarts?

ANSWERS

P:76–Q:1–Ans: Argus|

P:76–Q:2–Ans: Remus Lupin, Tonks and the Weasleys |

P:76–Q:3–Ans: Reg Cattermole |

P:76–Q:4–Ans: Dolores Umbridge |

P:77–Q:5–Ans: Brothers |

P:77–Q:6–Ans: Xenophilius Lovegood |

P:77–Q:7–Ans: Percy |

P:77–Q8–Ans: Seeker |

P:77–Q:9–Ans: The Quibbler |

P:78–Q:10–Ans: Draco Malfoy and Blaise Zabini |

P:78–Q:11–Ans: Durmstrang |

P:78–Q:12–Ans: Department of International Magical Co-Operation |

P:79–Q:13–Ans: Professor Snape |

P:79–Q:14–Ans: Professor Dumbledore |

P:79–Q:15–Ans: Jean |

P:79–Q:16–Ans: Ron Weasley |

P:79–Q:17–Ans: Severus Snape |

P80–Q:18–Ans: Holyhead Harpies |

P80–Q:19–Ans: Albus Severus Potter |

P80–Q:20–Ans: Wandmaker |

P80–Q:21–Ans: The Muggle Prime Minister |

P80–Q:22–Ans: He is an elf |

P81–Q:23–Ans: A doe |

P81–Q:24–Ans: Single-malt whiskey |

P81–Q:25–Ans: A Wrackspurt |

P81–Q:26–Ans: Giants & Acromantula |

P82–Q:27–Ans: Rollerskates |

P82–Q:28–Ans: Aragog |

P82–Q:29–Ans: Hedwig |

P82–Q:30–Ans: Grawp |

P82–Q:31–Ans: Kreacher |

P83–Q:32–Ans: A spider |

P83–Q:33–Ans: A werewolf |

P83–Q:34–Ans: Owls |

P83–Q:35–Ans: Inferi |

P84–Q:36–Ans: The Centaurs |

P84–Q:37–Ans: Laughter |

P84–Q:38–Ans: Eagle |

P84–Q:39–Ans: Dobby the elf |

P85–Q:40–Ans: Mrs Norris |

P85–Q:41–Ans: Toad |

P85–Q:42–Ans: A Hippogriff / Buckbeak |

P85–Q:43–Ans: A portkey |

P86–Q:44–Ans: Draco Malfoy |

P86–Q:45–Ans: Produces the Elixir of Life and turns any metal object into gold |

P86–Q:46–Ans: Flying motorbike |

P86–Q:47–Ans: Every-Flavour Beans |

P86–Q:48–Ans: A tail feather from the same phoenix |

P87–Q:49–Ans: The Tales of Beadle the Bard |

P87–Q:50–Ans: Dragon heart string |

P87–Q:51–Ans: Viewing memories |

P87–Q:52–Ans: Escape from Azkaban! |

P88–Q:53–Ans: Ron, Harry and Hermione |

P88–Q:54–Ans: Yes |

P88–Q:55–Ans: In a pink umbrella |

P88–Q:56–Ans: 'I open at the close' |

P89–Q:57–Ans: R.A.B |

P89–Q:58–Ans: The sword of Gryffindor |

P89–Q:59–Ans: Red |

P89–Q:60–Ans: Lily and James Potter, Sirius Black and Remus Lupin |

P89–Q:61–Ans: Filch's office |

P90–Q:62–Ans: An armchair |

P90–Q:63–Ans: A clock |

P90–Q:64–Ans: Alohomora |

P90–Q:65–Ans: Fred and George Weasley |

P91–Q:66–Ans: Stinging Jinx |

P91–Q:67–Ans: Professor Slughorn |

P91–Q:68–Ans: A strand of Bellatrix's hair |

P91–Q:69–Ans: Reducto |

P92–Q:70–Ans: Wingardium Leviosa |

P92–Q:71–Ans: The Patronus Charm |

P92–Q:72–Ans: Diffindo |

P92–Q:73–Ans: Invading someone's mind |

P93–Q:74–Ans: Obliviate |

P93–Q:75–Ans: Green |

P93–Q:76–Ans: Detecting when underage wizards use magic |

P93–Q:77–Ans: Gregory Goyle |

P93–Q:78–Ans: A cat |

P94–Q:79–Ans: Polyjuice potion to make everyone look like Harry |

P94–Q:80–Ans: Expelliramus |

P94–Q:81–Ans: Romilda Vane |

P94–Q:82–Ans: Bombarda |

You may also like other books in the unofficial

Harry Potter

series....

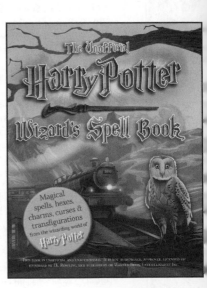

These books are unofficial and unauthorised. They are not authorised, approved, licensed or endorsed by J.K. Rowling, her publishers or Warner Bros. Entertainment Inc.